MISSION: SPECIAL OPS

GREEN BERETS

MISSION CRITICAL!

BY SARAH EASON
ILLUSTRATED BY DIEGO VIASBERG

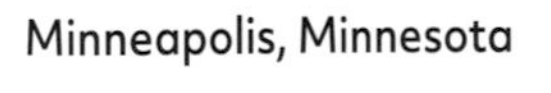
Minneapolis, Minnesota

Credits: 20, © Staff Sgt Elizabeth Pena/US Army; 21, © Staff Sgt Osvaldo Equite/US Dept of Defense; 22t, © Senior Airman Liliana Moreno/US Air Force; 22l, © SrA Colville McFee/Wikimedia Commons; 22b, © Get Military Photos/Shutterstock.

Editor: Jennifer Sanderson
Proofreader: Harriet McGregor
Designer: Paul Myerscough
Picture Researcher: Rachel Blount

DISCLAIMER: This graphic story is a dramatization based on true events. It is intended to give the reader a sense of the narrative rather than a presentation of actual details as they occurred.

Library of Congress Cataloging-in-Publication Data

Names: Eason, Sarah, author. | Viasberg, Diego, 1981- illustrator.
Title: Green Berets : mission critical! / by Sarah Eason ; illustrations by Diego Viasberg.
Description: Minneapolis, MN : Bearport Publishing Company, [2021] | Series: Mission: Special Ops | Includes bibliographical references and index.
Identifiers: LCCN 2020030827 (print) | LCCN 2020030828 (ebook) | ISBN 9781647476410 (library binding) | ISBN 9781647476489 (paperback) | ISBN 9781647476557 (ebook)
Subjects: LCSH: Iraq War, 2003-2011—Juvenile literature. | Iraq War, 2003-2011—Comic books, strips, etc. | United States. Army. Special Forces—Juvenile literature. | United States. Army. Special Forces—Comic books, strips, etc. | Good, Bernard Charles—Juvenile literature. | Good, Bernard Charles—Comic books, strips, etc. | LCGFT: Graphic novels.
Classification: LCC DS79.763 .E27 2021 (print) | LCC DS79.763 (ebook) | DDC 956.7044/342—dc23
LC record available at https://lccn.loc.gov/2020030827
LC ebook record available at https://lccn.loc.gov/2020030828

For more information, write to Bearport Publishing, 5357 Penn Avenue South, Minneapolis, MN 55419. Printed in the United States of America.

CONTENTS

CHAPTER ONE

ON PATROL

Among the U.S. soldiers in Iraq was an **elite** group called the Green Berets. On October 31, 2003, Sergeant Bernard Good and his 11-person team were on **patrol**.
STAY ALERT, TEAM!
The team was to carry out a **reconnaissance** mission in the town of Husaybah. Bernard's job was to watch for danger coming from behind the two-vehicle patrol group.
WE'RE HEADING BACK TO BASE NOW.
ROGER THAT!

Suddenly, a **rocket-propelled grenade (RPG)** was launched at the team.
WHOOSH!
IT'S AN RPG! GET DOWN!

Luckily, the grenade bounced off the truck and hit the ground.
PHEW, IT DIDN'T DO ANY DAMAGE.
THAT WAS A CLOSE CALL. CAN YOU SEE WHERE IT CAME FROM?

OVER THERE, LOOK!
WE'VE GOT EYES ON THE ATTACKERS. THEY ARE THREE MEN NORTH OF HERE.
TURN AROUND AND HEAD NORTH. WE NEED TO TRACK DOWN THE ATTACKERS.
ROGER, TURNING NOW!

UNDER FIRE

Bernard and fellow berets Joe Briscoe and Don Hogan grabbed hold of one of the attackers.
GOT HIM!
HOLD HIM DOWN!
THIS ONE IS SECURED! YOU GUYS HEAD AFTER THE OTHERS!
DON'T LOSE THEM!
QUICK! WE NEED TO GET THEM BEFORE THEY ESCAPE!

I'LL RADIO BASE TO TELL THEM WHAT HAS HAPPENED.

Just as Joe was radioing, the group found themselves under attack again. Heavy gunfire and more RPGs rained down on the men.
WHOOSH!
BOOM!

Bernard raced toward the attackers. He positioned himself between the gunfire and his team to try to hold off the enemy fire.

WE'VE GOT YOU COVERED, BERNARD.
AIM YOUR FIRE THERE!
ROGER THAT.

BANG!

AAH! I'VE BEEN HIT!

CHAPTER THREE

MAN DOWN!

Don gave Joe first aid while Bernard held off the enemy.

GET HIM IN THE TRUCK—WE'VE GOT TO GET HIM OUT OF HERE.
They drove straight into the enemy fire.
GET US OUT OF HERE!
ARGH!

I'M COMING! STAY WITH JOE, DON.

Bernard drove the truck toward the team's base camp.
HANG IN THERE, JOE. I'M GONNA GET YOU TO SAFETY.
Despite Bernard's best efforts, the gunfire was too much. Soon the truck was **disabled**.
ARGH! THIS TRUCK'S FINISHED!

WE'RE ONLY ABOUT 20 YARDS* FROM THE ROAD THAT LEADS TO CAMP.
I'M GOING TO GET JOE OUT. CAN YOU COVER ME?
NO PROBLEM! YOU JUST FOCUS ON GETTING HIM TO SAFETY.
* 18 m
GET HIM OUT OF HERE, DON. I'LL KEEP YOU COVERED!

CHAPTER FOUR

RESCUE MISSION

IT HURTS!

I KNOW, BUT I'VE GOTTA GET YOU OUT OF HERE.

HANG ON, JOE. WE'RE ALMOST THERE.

Just then, an Iraqi **civilian** drove down the road.

STOP! STOP!

The driver sped off with the Green Berets in the car and headed for their base camp. Gunfire rained down on them as they went.

WE'RE COMING TO GET YOU GUYS. JUST HANG IN THERE!

Bernard's brave actions in Iraq saved the life of Joe Briscoe and many other Green Berets. He was awarded a **Silver Star** by President George W. Bush for his **heroic** efforts.

GREEN BERETS

The Green Berets are an elite group in the U.S. Army. They take on some of the most dangerous missions in the world. Often, they fight from behind enemy lines. Many of their missions require them to move quickly from place to place. They free prisoners, destroy enemy weapons, and stop **terrorists** with speed and agility.

AS PART OF THEIR TRAINING, GREEN BERET SOLDIERS CARRY OUT FAKE MISSIONS FROM BLACK HAWK HELICOPTERS.

THE GREEN BERETS OFTEN TRAIN SPECIAL FORCES SOLDIERS IN OTHER COUNTRIES.

Berets are not only fighters but also teachers. In foreign lands, they help local citizens remove cruel rulers. They teach locals how to fight for themselves.

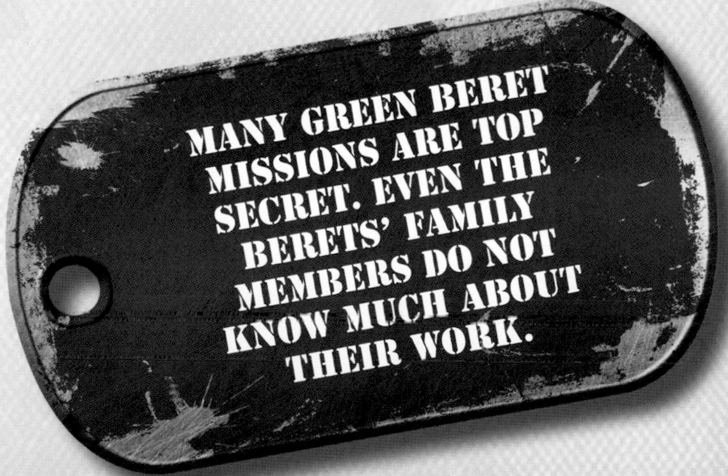

GREEN BERET GEAR

Berets use lots of equipment to carry out their missions. Here is some of the gear they use.

THE MC-5 PARACHUTE LETS GREEN BERETS JUMP INTO ENEMY AREAS.

THE ZODIAC INFLATABLE BOAT IS LIGHT AND EASY TO CARRY AND CAN BE USED FOR QUICK **TRANSITIONS** INTO WATER.

AN M4 CARBINE RIFLE IS ONE OF THE WEAPONS THE GREEN BERETS USE.

GLOSSARY

civilian a member of the general public who is not a part of the armed forces

disabled made unable to work properly

elite highly skilled

heroic very brave

invaded went into a country to take it over

patrol to move through an area to find out what is happening there

Quick Reaction Force a group of soldiers who are trained to react very quickly to difficult or dangerous situations

reconnaissance a military activity where soldiers are sent to gather information about something

rocket-propelled grenade (RPG) an explosive weapon that is fired using a rocket

secured under control

Silver Star a medal given to U.S. soldiers who have shown great bravery in battle

terrorists people who use violence to get attention and get other people to do what they want

transitions changes, for example, from a land mission to a water mission

weapons of mass destruction weapons, such as nuclear weapons, that have the potential to kill many people at once

INDEX

READ MORE

Manning, Matthew K. *U.S. Special Forces: Ghosts of the Night (Connect. U.S. Special Ops.)*. Mankato, MN: Capstone Publishing, 2017.

Simons, Lisa M. Bolt. *U.S. Army Green Beret Missions: A Timeline (Blazers. Special Ops Mission Timelines)*. Mankato, MN: Capstone Publishing, 2016.

Yomtov, Nel. *Special Ops (Epic Military Missions)*. Minneapolis: Bellwether Media, 2017.

LEARN MORE ONLINE

1. Go to **www.factsurfer.com**
2. Enter **"Mission Critical"** into the search box.
3. Click on the cover of this book to see a list of websites.